LIVING WITH A TBI
(Traumatic Brain Injury)
From My Perspective

BEAU BAKER

TRILOGY

Trilogy Christian Publishers
A Wholly Owned Subsidiary of Trinity Broadcasting Network
2442 Michelle Drive
Tustin, CA 92780

Copyright © 2021 by Beau Baker

Scripture quotations marked KJV are taken from the King James Version of the Bible. Public domain.

No part of this book may be reproduced, stored in a retrieval system, or transmitted by any means without written permission from the author. All rights reserved.

Cover design by: Cornerstone Creative Solutions

For information, address Trilogy Christian Publishing
Rights Department, 2442 Michelle Drive, Tustin, Ca 92780.
Trilogy Christian Publishing/ TBN and colophon are trademarks of Trinity Broadcasting Network.

For information about special discounts for bulk purchases, please contact Trilogy Christian Publishing.

Manufactured in the United States of America

Trilogy Disclaimer: The views and content expressed in this book are those of the author and may not necessarily reflect the views and doctrine of Trilogy Christian Publishing or the Trinity Broadcasting Network.

10 9 8 7 6 5 4 3 2 1

Library of Congress Cataloging-in-Publication Data is available.

ISBN 978-1-63769-268-4 (Print Book)
ISBN 978-1-63769-269-1 (ebook)

DEDICATION

This book is dedicated and written in loving memory of my grandmother, Ruth Courey, who played a major role in helping me not give up on myself but to instead keep pursuing God's perfect plan for my life. She will always be remembered for her sweet, kind, and loving spirit that touched so many people.

CONTENTS

Introduction 7

Chapter One: Life Before the TBI 9

Chapter Two: Transitioning to College 19

Chapter Three: The Injury and the Detour 25

Chapter Four: The TBI and Life Changing Impacts 31

Chapter Five: The Long Slow Road to Recovery 41

Chapter Six: Getting Back in School Mode 49

Chapter Seven: Graduation and Volunteering 55

Chapter Eight: Master's Degree and Work 61

Chapter Nine: Success at Work and Personal Life 69

Chapter Ten: COVID-19 and a New Venture 77

Chapter Eleven: Hopes for the Future 81

Conclusion 85

INTRODUCTION

SUFFERING A TRAUMATIC brain injury (TBI) is devastating for the individual as well as the family members, friends, and any care takers involved. Most people would tell you "just give it some time to mend and you will be fine," but the reality is far from that. The severity of the injury can play a significant impact, and in many cases causes the victim to have to re-learn many things over again from the very beginning. There is more to learn about a TBI than just considering it a minor concussion-like symptom. In my case, I experienced a frontal lobe brain injury, which directly affects one's daily executive functioning.

Becoming properly educated about the causes, effects, and long-term considerations for someone living with a TBI should be advocated more throughout hospital settings as well as health education environments. Having a better perspective and understanding of people living with traumatic brain injuries could play an important role in the etiquette levels of those trying to work with and relate to a person with a TBI. Many times, people are ignorant and do not understand how to properly conduct themselves in a setting that has one or more individuals who have a TBI. They can be acquired neurologically at birth or be the result from things such as car accidents, work-related injuries, sports, daily living/recreational activities, serving in the military, or other.

Listening to stories from survivors of a traumatic brain injury can tremendously impact others by creating awareness, along with learning what it means to empathize. It can truly humble the attitudes of many. Living with a TBI in many ways can be frustrating; but at the same time, it can be rewarding depending on how the perception of the individual is depicted. After reading the highlighted documentary, you should walk away with a little better understanding of what it is like living in the shoes of someone who has a TBI.

CHAPTER ONE

Life Before the TBI

GROWING UP AS an only child in the loving home of two wonderful parents who taught me the basic principles of living a Christian lifestyle from an early age on was the cornerstone foundation to where I am at in life now. From kindergarten through eighth grade, I attended a private Christian school in St. Augustine, Florida. From the very beginning at five years old, I was introduced to the unconditional love of Jesus Christ and the free gift of eternal life and salvation that is readily available to whosoever believes in Him. Knowing this powerful truth is what has stayed with me and kept me going today! "Train up a child in the way he should go, and when he is old, he will not depart from it" (Proverbs 22:6, KJV).

Living my daily life for Jesus and being taught about God's Word at school was deeply rooted within me and has not departed, no matter how far I seemed to have run away. What I realize now is that God never stopped loving me and never let go of me. Memorizing Bible verses, taking tests, and performing in plays replicating Biblical stories gave me up-close and personal revelational knowledge of God from early on. The school (Trinity Chapel Christian School) which I attended gave me an overall experience of what the love of Jesus is all about. God's love is chasing after all of us whether we realize it or not, and He has His arms open wide, waiting for anyone who is willing to begin a personal relationship with Him by believing in His son Jesus Christ. "By confessing with your mouth that Jesus is Lord and believing in your heart that God raised Him from the dead after shedding His blood on the cross for our sins," the Bible says you will be saved (Romans 10:9, KJV).

Having parents who were actively involved in every area of my upbringing gave me the mental edge I needed to succeed both academically and athletically. My priorities were instilled in me to ensure that I would act like a responsible young man and be respectful to all my elders. Making it a habit to study the Bible, get all my homework completed on time, and practice sports at the same time—which happened to primarily be basketball and Taekwondo—was how I functioned. Knowing that I had a mom and dad who would attend all my events gave me overwhelming confidence to perform at a high level because of the support they showered me with. Ultimately, with God's loving mercy and grace, along with the love and support from my parents, I am standing stronger than ever today!

As I got older, the dream continued of being a diligent student making outstanding grades while balancing the ability to thrive in sports. Being a very introverted and extremely shy kid had its advantages and disadvantages when I was younger. I was born with OCD and later developed social anxiety disorder. Feeling awkward along with intimidation at times in social situations gave me a reason to keep quiet and provide a word or two feedback when people tried to engage me in conversation. This continued all throughout my adolescence and early adulthood. The fortunate thing for me was the fact that I excelled in sports, particularly basketball and Taekwondo during those years, which gave me an outlet from many people knowing who I was. As the years passed by, it was always a good feeling when other people who knew of me because of my athletic abilities and accomplishments always did the talking for me, even though I had no clue who they were.

This feeling of other people knowing me through my outstanding athletic achievements made me feel famous and important. It was truly a humbling experience that was extremely gratifying, which still I never forget to this day. Even though I could have let my ego take over and think I was better than everyone else, the gentle and humble heart the Lord instilled in me kept me grounded. My preparation and study habits remained steady in all facets of my life because God was directing my steps. Earning high academic honors in school while winning numerous awards on the basketball court and in Taekwondo gave me the confidence I needed to keep pressing forward. In doing all these things, God was at the center of my life, as were my parents, being the caring, loving, and supportive people they were.

When I was in my final year of middle school, I was excited to know all the hard work had paid off, and I would be graduating from Trinity Chapel Christian School.

My mental attitude was extremely high focused on growing my relationship with Jesus and excelling at my academic studies, as well as at basketball and Taekwondo. Having this mindset to begin the school year set me up for a year of success and lasting memories. During my eighth-grade year, I did very well maintaining my grades by prioritizing my Bible study time, keeping up with all my homework, playing on two basketball teams—school team and county league—

and practicing as often as possible with both basketball and Taekwondo. It was an awesome feeling to know that because of the loving grace and mercy of God, I was thriving and on pace to graduate with honors. I would be a vessel of worship for the Lord in the future to come. The basketball season was great because during my middle school years I played on the school team and for the county recreation league. Earning the most valuable player award for both teams as well as holding a straight A average in school was a humbling experience. It propelled me to finish out the rest of the school year strongly and graduate valedictorian from the only school I had ever known up until that point.

When reality finally set in after my final day at Trinity Chapel Christian School that year, I was excited and looking forward to the next chapter of my life by starting high school in the next few months. All throughout my elementary and middle school years, I had neighborhood friends as well as people I knew through playing sports that I was close with. Since there was not a high school offered yet at Trinity Chapel Christian School where I previously attended, the decision to choose a high school was tough. I had a few options, but in the end, I chose St. Augustine High School, which was a public high school. I was excited to begin this new chapter of my life knowing that I had neighborhood friends as well as other friends that I grew up with who would be going to the same public high school. As the summer began to wind down that year in 1998, I was preparing for the transition that would be one of the most eye-opening in my life up to that point.

Starting my first year of high school was exciting for me! This would be the first year in my life that I would be attending a public school, and I knew there would be some significant differences. It did not take long before I noticed the changes in how students interacted with one another and the respect level they had for teachers and faculty. I was raised by my parents and brought up in a private Christian school setting. The behavior of public high school students was completely disrespectful and intimidating to me. It took several weeks to months of adjustment and transition, but I was able to adapt over time.

Even though I adapted to the new environment, I remained an introvert and rarely said much to anyone. This was not because I was arrogant and thought highly of myself; it was because I was very shy and felt awkward in social situations. Thinking of what others might say about me or how they would respond was what held me back from engaging in communication with others. This was a bad excuse considering that God was always for us and fought all our battles. If I would have meditated more on God's Word back then, I would have reached out to others and been friendlier to my peers. This would have given me many more opportunities to let my light shine brightly for Jesus Christ when in the school setting. However, I was always very shy and sensitive as to how someone would perceive me.

When I was involved in sports, both basketball and Taekwondo, it was almost like I was in a zone that persisted with intense focus on the activity at hand. Playing basketball my entire life made it an easy decision for me to try out for the high school basketball team. There was a lot of talent at St. Augustine High School at the time because all the other county schools had not yet opened to rezone many of the students that would later depart at the end of the year. Making the freshman team my first year ended up alright because it gave me experience to build upon for the years to come. Both basketball and Taekwondo went very well, and I was able to maintain good grades my first year at the public high school.

Looking back, the one thing that kept me from being a true leader and classified in the elite category for basketball and Taekwondo was my lack of communication skills. Had I been able to effectively communicate with my coaches and teammates, I would have been one of the top star players in the county. The ability and skill levels for both sports were there from the beginning, and if it were just based on that alone, I was recognized by many people everywhere I went. In my own evaluation, my freshman and sophomore years were limited to the freshman and junior varsity teams because of my inability to be more vocal. Statistically, both years were productive, and I dominated the basketball court, which gave me a stronger confidence level going into my junior year.

Prior to starting my freshman year of high school, I excelled in the Korean form of martial arts (Taekwondo) and took my junior black belt examination before I started school. Junior black belts were given to students age sixteen and younger. I knew I was more than ready to earn my first-degree black belt. When the examination came, I performed well on all the required forms, self-defense techniques, sparring, and individual testing panel questionnaire. At the conclusion, my family and I thought I passed with flying colors, but because the fellow students in my class were not at the same level as myself and did poorly, the judges decided to fail all the Taekwondo participants being tested that day. It was upsetting because of the disappointing news I received from my instructor. He said, "Beau, you did not pass. Not because of anything you did wrong. In fact, you should have passed your black belt test today, but because of your fellow students not being prepared and failing, the judges decided not to pass (you) one student, but rather fail the entire group." This was devastating news for me and crushed my ego and confidence level. Shortly after this, I decided to stop taking Taekwondo to pursue basketball with all my attention and focus.

Making this decision helped my concentration level and kept me dedicated to the game that I have loved since being a little boy. With Taekwondo being put to the side and my junior year approaching soon, I was consistently practicing my basketball skills and training hard to be fully prepared when the season arrived. Having the extra time helped me psychologically to put all my effort into being the best basketball player that I could possibly be. It sure paid off because the year before I had put on a lot of weight, and this gave me a reason to make sure I was properly conditioned for the upcoming season. The consistency, dedication, and hard work paid off come time for varsity basketball tryouts because it put me at a level that no one else could keep up with, which was self-rewarding. My conditioning and skill levels were superior to my other peers, and this was the beginning to a fantastic final two years of high school basketball. The team always looked to me for scoring and to take and make the winning shots.

Completing my first two years of high school was exciting, knowing that I was halfway there but the competitive side of me still had more things to accomplish. Making the varsity basketball team my junior year was good, and I knew that it was time to shine on the court. The opportunities were there as I had a decent season statistically and collectively as a part of the team, but the lack of communication on my behalf to teammates and coaches is what hindered my abilities to dominate the court and thrive at an elite level. Relying solely on my basketball abilities and talents to do the talking for me worked for a while, but to reach a higher status, I needed to communicate better with people in general.

Before I knew it, I was entering my senior year with a lot of hype on the upcoming basketball season. My grades were maintained at a high level, the passion to excel on the basketball court was there, and finally it was time to put all the drive and effort into the season. The very first game of the season was a thriller, with us losing in overtime to our cross-town rival. My statistics were superb and continued to be throughout the year, which was very humbling being that I made many shots that ultimately won many of my team's games. I was being congratulated by people at just about every gymnasium I played in. My parents attended every game and various family members would occasionally attend games to give me support, and this always meant a lot to me. As the season finished up and school year ended, another chapter in my life would soon be completed when I attended my public high school graduation ceremony at the University of North Florida campus in Jacksonville, Florida.

CHAPTER TWO

Transitioning to College

MY LIFE HAD been wonderful so far, and I was ready to move away from home to live in the college dorm at Palm Beach Atlantic University, where I had decided to attend school and play basketball. This transition was tough on my parents, especially my mom because I was an only child. Living on-campus was convenient being there was a cafeteria to eat all my meals, a student union, recreation center, and lots of other amenities offered to students. The food was exceptional, classes went well, and basketball practice was off to a good start. My parents were happy knowing I was in a Christian university.

Everything seemed to be going well my first college semester living away from home until my roommate and next-door neighbor in the dorm started influencing me in extremely negative ways. My roommate was several years older than me and was a bartender at the local Chilis restaurant in town. The next-door dorm neighbor smoked and had a few loose screws, to say the least. It was not the ideal pairing that I should have ended up with, but in retrospect it has all worked out as part of God's plan for my life and for

His glory! My roommate Kelly told me he had been recently released from prison for grand theft auto, not to mention he was several years older than me. His father was a pastor somewhere in Florida and was hoping PBAU would reform him. I believed the school's pairing of roommates was unfair to me, coming in at eighteen years old, shy, and naïve. It was not a good match. When my roommate Kelly would come back to the dorm late at night after work and bring his alcohol to store it in our small dorm room refrigerator, the noise would wake me up from sleeping. This persisted along with the pornography he would watch on our shared dorm room computer while trying to convince me with his bullying tactics to sit with him and watch it. With all the sporadic occurrences that took place over my first year of college, the effects of it all came to light when I started missing early morning practices for the basketball team.

Due to my introverted nature combined with all the distractions from my roommate and neighbor, the basketball coach was concerned because I was missing practice. I was an invited walk-on, and the behavior I was engaging in was detrimental to my success both academically and athletically. My mother received a phone call one evening from my basketball coach stating I had missed many practices and would be released from the team if I did not start showing up. My parents were shocked to hear this news; they had no idea of my behavior, what had become of me, and how I was being influenced by my roommate and next-door dorm neighbor. Not too long after, the incidents started diminishing, and I was getting back on the right track. Having away games where we traveled to different cities and states was exciting. Flying to Boston, Massachusetts for a tournament was the most interesting trip of the season. All in all, the season was an average one record-wise, and now it was time for me to finish up the academic semester and make some decisions for the upcoming future.

Before the first fall semester ended, my roommate Kelly and neighbor David peer-pressured me into going downtown to a night club. You had to be eighteen to enter and twenty-one or older to drink. I had never in my life been around or considered engaging in this type of behavior, but suddenly it was becoming a reality. Some of the upper classmen on the basketball team were there, and I felt out of place to be honest. Seeing this environment for the first time shocked me because I did not know what to expect and how to handle myself around drunk and high individuals saying crazy things while acting completely foolish. This was all a new shock to my system, but I felt pressured into engaging in this lifestyle so my teammates and roommate would not make fun of me and think I was an outcast or a goody-goody two shoes. I always felt inferior and bullied, but too shy to speak up and just say, "No!" Ultimately, both my roommate and next-door dorm neighbor were kicked out of PBAU.

After these events took place, I had a lot of different things to think about for the remainder of the school year. As the semester began to wind down with final exams quickly approaching, I was able to study and successfully complete my freshman year of college. When my parents arrived on campus to help me move out of the dorms, I was eager to get going as fast as we could. It was a difficult summer to deal with several issues; that made me really think hard about where the next steps of my future would take place. Transferring schools, trying out for a new basketball team, and renewing my mind with God's Word were the main concerns to figure out before the next school year began. The trip from Palm Beach Atlantic University was 250 miles to where

I lived in St. Augustine, Florida; so, it was not bad at all, and I was happy to be home for the summer.

During the summer of 2003, my parents and I thought of the best possible options for me regarding the upcoming school year, where to play basketball, and how to keep God first place in every area of my life. A good option that came to mind was to stay locally in St. Augustine and attend the community college until I earned my two-year AA degree. My dad ended up contacting the head basketball coach for the school and arranged for me to participate in an open try-out for the team. This had me excited to possibly play for a new school and have all my transcripts sent to the college so that I could then sign up for fall classes. Everything seemed to be taken care of, and I was looking forward to the fresh start. That summer I did my best to practice diligently and train hard to make a good impression on the basketball court when I had the tryout.

The day of the tryout was here, and I was prepared to give it my best effort. Upon arrival to the campus, my dad and I walked into the gym and saw some sort of unorganized pick-up basketball taking place. The coach picked teams a little while after with me getting my first chance to play, and the game was no different than playing a wild, out of control game at the park. About halfway into the game, I came down the court, received the ball, made a drive to the basket, and was knocked down hard to the floor by an opposing player. I lay there for a little bit while the game continued, and the coach yelled, "Are you going to play or not?" This sparked me to get up and keep playing, despite the pain in my wrist. I finished the game and left the gym with my dad, having no pain in my wrist the entire ride home. That night when the swelling and throbbing pain began, I woke up in the middle of the night and had to put ice on my wrist because it got so bad. The pain was unbearable, and my competitive basketball career was on the decline. In the morning, after being awake most of the night because of the pain and swelling, my parents and I decided to go to the emergency room.

Once at the hospital and after the MRI, it was confirmed that I had broken the scaphoid bone in my left wrist. All the hospital could do was put a sling on my arm and recommend me to visit the orthopedic office for casting and further diagnosis. When I visited the orthopedic doctor, he confirmed I had a broken scaphoid bone and scheduled me to get a full arm cast for total immobilization. This was a devastating blow to my psyche, and all the confidence I had was drained out of me in a matter of seconds. Knowing that I would have to wear a full-arm cast for several months followed by a short-arm cast for a few weeks was devastating news. The hopeful basketball tryout and future that I had in collegiate athletics was all but over. I realized that God and school should be my top two priorities in that order.

CHAPTER THREE

The Injury and the Detour

THE CAST WAS on my left arm now and I was starting classes locally in St. Augustine, Florida at St. Johns River Community College. It was reassuring knowing that I was close to home and knew the town backwards and forwards since I had lived there my entire life. Classes went well, the healing process was off to a good start, and my life had taken a small detour for now compared to the big one that would be coming several years down the road. Not being able to do the things that I loved so much such as exercising, playing basketball and other sports, and going swimming at the beach (to name a few) were reasons that put me in a depressed mental state for quite a while. Living back home, I had several friends around town who went to high school with me that liked to get together when all of us were available.

The activities I had previously been exposed to from a former college roommate and neighbor while away at Palm Beach Atlantic University would later come back to haunt me and take control of my life for the worst after a near fatal car accident in 2009. My parents did all they could to talk to me about not drinking, the effects of drinking and driving, and how it destroyed your brain cells, but I was stubborn, thought I knew more than them, and would not listen.

Every day that went by seemed like an eternity with the cast on my arm and the restrictions that kept me from doing many things. Several people signed my cast and wrote get well messages on it, which was nice because it gave me a little extra motivation. My grades were fine at school, and there were not any problems with the healing process, which was going along nicely according to schedule. Moving forward, I finished my two-year Associate of Arts Degree and now needed to transfer to a four-year institution to finish up with my bachelor's degree. The full arm cast was now condensed to a short arm cast mid forearm, and I was just a few short weeks away from completing the recovery process. I was eager to have the cast off for good and to also select a school to finish up my degree at. After several family discussions weighing out all the different options, we decided that I could finish up my degree at the University of Florida in Gainesville. My father was a graduate of the University of Florida and played baseball there. He was a UF letterman and proud that I was accepted to the same school he graduated from.

Knowing a few friends that attended University of Florida, along with the fact I grew up an avid Gator fan because my dad had played baseball there when he was in college, were determining factors in the decision. A high school friend of mine attending UF lived in a house off campus and had an extra room for rent. That summer my parents and I packed all my belongings, and I moved away from home off to college for the second time to Gainesville, Florida. This was exciting because, as it turned out, there were two high school guys I knew who would be living with me. The move went smoothly; my cast had been off for a while by then, and I was all registered and ready to start fall classes in the new environment. As a shy guy along with being a believer in Jesus Christ as my Lord and Savior, the next several years of my life would be difficult in a sense that I would face a lot of peer pressure once again, this time in a college party town atmosphere.

The first semester was fine, but I could tell early on that there were going to be a lot of distractions trying to lure me away from being a successful student. Learning the new culture and seeing firsthand some of the behavior of students on campus and around town was plenty to absorb my first few months living away from home. It was the following spring semester when I turned twenty-one years old that I started noticing myself fall off track and give into the temptations of drinking and partying. This behavior began to slowly spiral more and more out of control with my friends and other acquaintances encouraging me to outdrink everyone and be the life of every party. My shy personality combined with an overabundance of alcohol made me feel on top of the world, but unfortunately this lifestyle would repeatedly continue until the night of my near fatal car accident.

Time after time, I would drink myself to oblivion and frequently make a fool of myself wherever I was for the occasion. I realize now I was just the town's clown. The group that was along with me—usually consisting of my roommates and a few other friends—tried to calm me down, but I would persist on drinking and socializing with whoever was there. After every party or social drinking event, I would get taken advantage of by driving everyone home but first stopping at a late-night restaurant and picking up the tab for everyone. This became a regular occurrence because I was too weak to say no to them and make someone else drive. My desire of wanting to be socially accepted by my friends and liked by them was stronger that my willpower to make boundaries for myself and, most importantly, to put God first. Through it all, I have learned an enormous amount of valuable life lessons. I realize now few of my friends were truly genuine and caring. They were only interested in seeing me make a fool of myself so they could all laugh at me while taking advantage of me driving them places and always paying for their restaurant meals.

From waking up in my jeep to passing out and vomiting in a random person's bathroom at a party, I experienced just about every scene imaginable back in those days. Although I had been to all the bars, clubs, and house parties, this was not a proud confession to make because my life was spinning out of control while losing grip on my priorities and what should have been valued as top importance to me. Once again taking me back to high school memories, I lacked the ability to effectively communicate to my peers and put God first along with my academic priorities ahead of making friends happy. Time continued to pass by, and my interest in promiscuous behaviors continued to override my reasons for being there. Now that I already had experience from my last college's lifestyle, along with all the new adventures in Gainesville, my immunity level was getting higher and higher to tolerate excessive amounts of alcohol while putting myself in unfavorable situations.

Being the joke among all my peers as well as others in attendance when we were out and about partying was normal to me. Whenever someone dared me to do something, I would be the first to act because I valued having the approval of others more so than wanting the approval of God. It was an incredibly sad situation in the sense that I had my core values, focus, and number one priority being Jesus Christ out of order, which was leading me in the direction of a desert valley that Satan was deceiving and luring me towards. I was backslidden. With no other strong-willed Christian believers around that could connect with me to help the issue, my mind continued to absorb all the comments from peers that distracted me from God's Word. The devil was the greatest enemy that I had with all the strongholds developed in my mind about being a people pleaser and chasing after the worldly desires instead of dying to my flesh and being alive to Jesus.

The worst part of all was when the negative behaviors carried over back home when I would return for breaks. Being a regular at all of St. Augustine's bars, along with branching off even further to large house parties after closing out the bars, was a regular routine of mine. My social anxiety around people contributed to me starting to purchase several twelve packs of beer and usually some type of alcohol to prime my system to get a buzz or high before attending any event. I would normally consume ten to twelve beers and some alcohol ahead of going out for the night. For most people, this would have been the stopping point, but for me it was just the beginning. I was born with OCD (obsessive compulsive behavior), so it was even more difficult for me to know when to stop. I was on prescription medication for my OCD but had stopped taking it when I found relief in alcohol. It removed all my inhibitions, and I felt like people accepted me because I was funny and much more talkative. My days and nights were all messed up with my bad habits. Being a high-volume binge drinker, I would start drinking around 4 or 5 p.m., with the event typically starting around 9 or 10 p.m. and going until 4 or 5 a.m. To make matters worse, friends or acquaintances had to nearly fight me to not drive on my own to various places. This pattern gradually got worse and worse over time leading up to my near-death experience that has forever changed my life for the best!

It is now that I realize God takes what the enemy means for evil and turns it to good. Since my automobile accident, I no longer need the crutches of alcohol to help me socialize and talk to people. I use my accident as a testimony to help other people going through the same addictions in life to show them God is real; He is alive, and He never fails. He is always with me and makes a way when there seems to be no way. Only Jesus can turn a mess into a message, a test into a testimony, a trial into a triumph, and a victim into a victory! He is worthy to be praised.

CHAPTER FOUR

The TBI and Life Changing Impacts

IN MY PRE-ACCIDENT days, as my life continually drifted further and further away from God, I found myself really enjoying the lifestyle I was living. This was the sad part, because putting my faith in Jesus Christ as Lord and Savior of my life was not the number one priority anymore. It came to be that pleasing others along with being selfish and wanting to gain all the attention from my bad behavior was controlling my life. This needed to stop, but my mind was set on the wrong things instead of my heart being focused on God as top priority.

The drinking habits continued along with the out-of-control party lifestyle. Going to all different types of bars, clubs, and house gatherings led to my dependency of alcohol instead of having my eyes fixed on Jesus Christ—with Him being the one I am most dependent upon. Every time I knew of a party or function to attend, I would drown myself in beer and alcohol before going because it would loosen me up to the point where I had no problem communicating with others. Time after time, the ritual I had of consuming way too much liquor before going out was getting out of hand, and if something bad happened because of my actions, it would not be a surprise as to why it happened. Deep down in my soul, I knew this lifestyle was not pleasing to God, and that was the displeasing feeling that was unfortunately overridden by my selfish desire to make other people happy. I let my flesh take over my spirit man.

My life was not moving in the right direction because of my choices, and God was trying the entire time to draw me back into His loving arms with the awesome purpose He has for my life. Many people who used to know me for the shy and reserved person I was, were now seeing the wild party side of me. I was starting to be recognized for the wrong reasons, but in my mind this attention was building my ego. Most people wanted to talk to me, which ultimately led to the increasing of my alcohol consumption. Later, I realized these so-called friends were laughing at me, not with me. This faulty thought pattern was what led to my downward spiral, which was what seemed like a domino effect and brought me literally crashing to pieces the night of September 18th, 2009, when my automobile accident occurred. Countless times, I would end up passed out in my vehicle either at some odd location or, by the grace of God, make it all the way in my driveway at home only to have to be awakened from a blacked-out state in the driver seat. This persisted all the way to the day of my life changing event, which had forever changed me for the best!

On September 17th, 2009, I was priming myself up for a local weekly event at one of the bars in St. Augustine. It was just another chance for me to act like a fool and then follow the crowd to the next popular location afterward. As usual, I drank heavily at the first bar and was ready to travel over to the next destination. Some people offered to drive me, but I refused and stubbornly got into my own vehicle to make the trip to the bar on Anastasia Island in St. Augustine Beach. This was more of a club type atmosphere with the upper-level deck being the music playing area with dancing and closer social interactions with alcohol being served on both levels. By this time of night, I was already overly intoxicated and talking to whoever came in close proximity. I did a couple of dances to the music, made my final rounds to say my goodbyes to people I knew, and then remembered waiting for the last call of alcohol and closing time. Being totally intoxicated and stumbling down the stairs across the street to my jeep in the parking lot was the last recollection I have of anything that took place prior to my vehicle crashing in downtown St. Augustine, Florida.

My journey back home started off the same as usual, with my stereo being set at full blast and having some type of hip-hop or rap music playing. The windows were down to act cool, along with wanting the attention. Shortly after I began driving, I noticed my head nodding a little with my eyes wanting to close. This was a normal procedure to me just as every other ride home had been in the past after a long night out drinking and partying. As I progressed towards the Bridge of Lions and downtown St. Augustine, my awareness continued fading in and out until finally I blacked out before losing control of my jeep and crashing. According to records, I hit the sidewall of the bridge, which caused my right rear tire to fall off. This caused my vehicle to speed up, and my jeep eventually flipped three or four times over the median, which resulted in me being ejected from the passenger side window because I was not wearing a seat belt. This was the beginning of a horrific, traumatic, life changing event that has forever changed my life for the better by bringing me back home to serve my Lord and Savior Jesus Christ and fulfill the true purpose that He has for me.

    Luckily, there was an officer parked in the downtown St. Augustine Square that witnessed the crash and called paramedics out to the scene immediately. Upon arrival, I was transported to Flagler Hospital located in St. Augustine, but because they do not have a trauma center, I was then air-lifted by helicopter to Shands Hospital in Jacksonville, Florida. The damage to my body from the impact of the crash had already been done, and it was now up to the medical professionals to give their best effort to restore my life. I was placed in the surgical intensive care unit with tubes hooked up all over my body and major decisions to be made regarding surgical procedures to be done. The trauma unit nurses repeatedly told my parents that every second counted. Later, the surgical procedures necessary were a tracheostomy for my windpipe and a fiberoptic monitor that needed to be inserted into the frontal lobe of my brain to relieve intracranial pressure. If that pressure would have risen to a certain level, surgery would have been needed. This would have involved removing a piece of my skull. Thank you, Lord, that this never happened!

The worst night of my parent's lives was about to take place early in the morning on Friday, September 18th, 2009. A knock on the door woke them up, and a police officer urged them to get to Shands Hospital quickly because their son had been air-lifted with life threatening injuries. They both panicked and instantly cried out to the Lord. Then they made the long drive to Shands Hospital, and upon arrival, they were immediately greeted by a chaplain at the emergency entrance. This was extremely disturbing since in most cases a chaplain is there to comfort and console the family members of a patient by praying with them. My parents panicked and wanted to know where I was and if I was okay. All the chaplain told them was that it was a profoundly serious accident, and all they could do was pray.

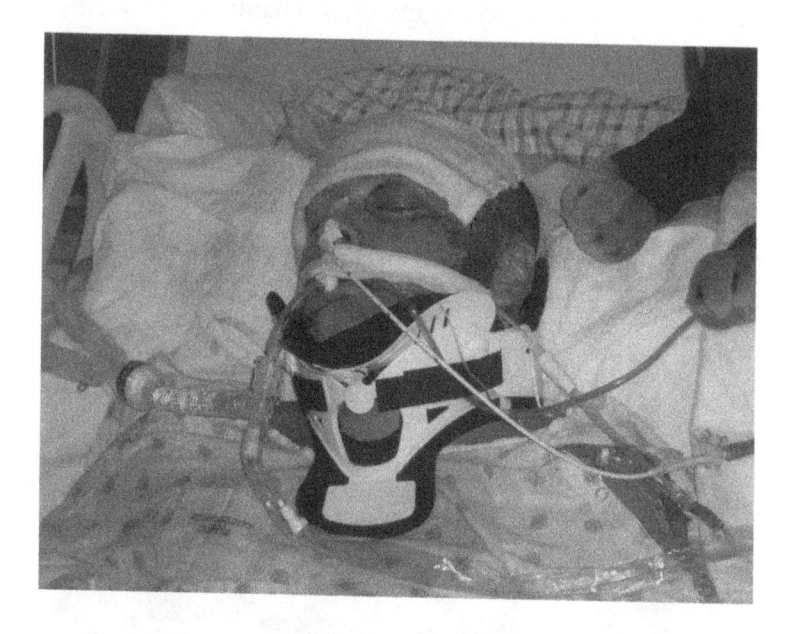

The tension levels were high, and for nearly two months my parents were there by my side in the hospital's surgical intensive care ward as I lay unconscious and in a coma, with tubes and ventilators connected. Initially doctors did not think I was going to survive beyond four hours at the most, and if so, I would be in a vegetative state for the rest of my life. With the swelling rising, my eye closed due to a hematoma, and my body in a completely broken state, the only true answer for my healing came from God. I suffered multiple broken bones, facial fractures, swelling of the brain, hematoma in my eye, bleeding from both ear canals, and both of my lungs were collapsed. My parents called family members, and soon prayer warriors from all over began praying and seeking God on my behalf for a miracle healing from this traumatic injury. To this day, I am still learning of more and more people who had me on their prayer lists from churches to friends and relatives. For the duration of the coma, doctors, nurses, and medical staff did a phenomenal job of caring for me, performing the necessary surgeries and being emotionally supportive to my parents. God's hands were all over my hospital room with His angels being in the form of all the helping hands involved in the surgical intensive care unit.

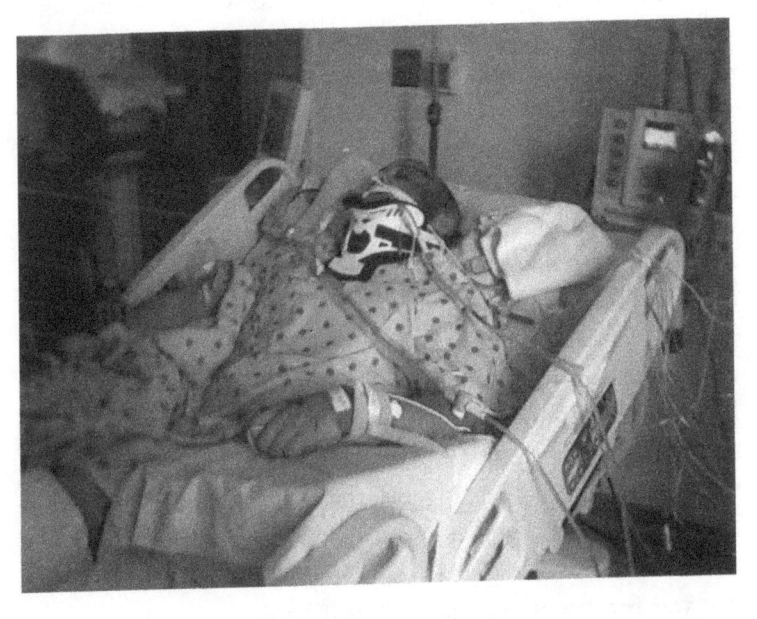

Countless days were spent visiting me and then sleeping in the waiting room when visitation hours were over. My parents were true warriors ignited with God's supernatural strength to be able to endure and withstand such horrible hardship and pain, not knowing what the final outcome would be. From making my room into an animal farm with numerous stuffed animals to my mother singing me hymns and songs and quietly talking to me while holding my one hand, both my parents kept an optimistic attitude despite the negative reports from the doctors. Having faith in Jesus was what gave them hope in the middle of the storm; in the long run, it was the persistent trust in the Lord that everything would be okay. Amidst the struggle, God saw their hurt, but more importantly, He recognized the unwavering faith in Jesus they had as the rock and firm foundation that would come through. All the credit, glory, honor, and praise belonged to my Lord and Savior Jesus, as well as the miraculous healing power that was all made possible to me because of the ultimate sacrifice He made on the cross for our sins.

Though each day spent in the surgical intensive care unit was agonizing for my entire family, God's plan and purpose remained with tiny bits of progress being made every day. When the time had come for me to be discharged from Shands Hospital and admitted over to Brooks Rehabilitation Hospital in Jacksonville, Florida, where I would need a lot of physical and cognitive rehabilitation, I was still not aware of my surroundings and what was taking place. For a while, I was told for safety precautions that I was placed in a zip up tent covering my bed to prevent me from getting out of the hospital bed. To this day, I have no recollection of this happening, which is a good thing because it would have been frustrating to know that I was being held in lockdown, even if it was for my own safety and well-being.

When I was aware of my surroundings and came to the realization that I was partially paralyzed on the left side of my body, the negative thoughts and strongholds of Satan began to register in my mind. Every day was a struggle to do the simple things in life that I once overlooked because I thought

I was invincible to the bad stuff. Over the years, my ego had become so elevated in an arrogant, conceited way where I thought I was immune to accidents and the life-threatening injuries you heard and read about. Being in the hospital firsthand was a big wake-up call for me, especially when I realized the use of my limbs had been restricted to absolute minimal movement. My psyche was deflated when I witnessed these things, and even though I had Jesus living in my heart as a born-again believer, the human side of me full of doubt and disbelief took over with Satan telling me lies about my future. The enemy gave me thoughts about ending my life and that my life was worthless now because I messed up so badly with my own stupid decisions.

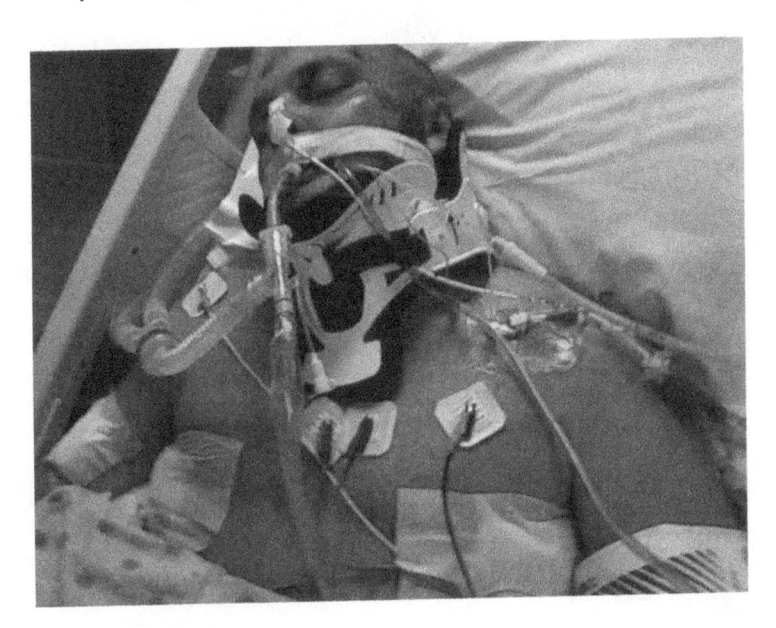

CHAPTER FIVE

The Long Slow Road to Recovery

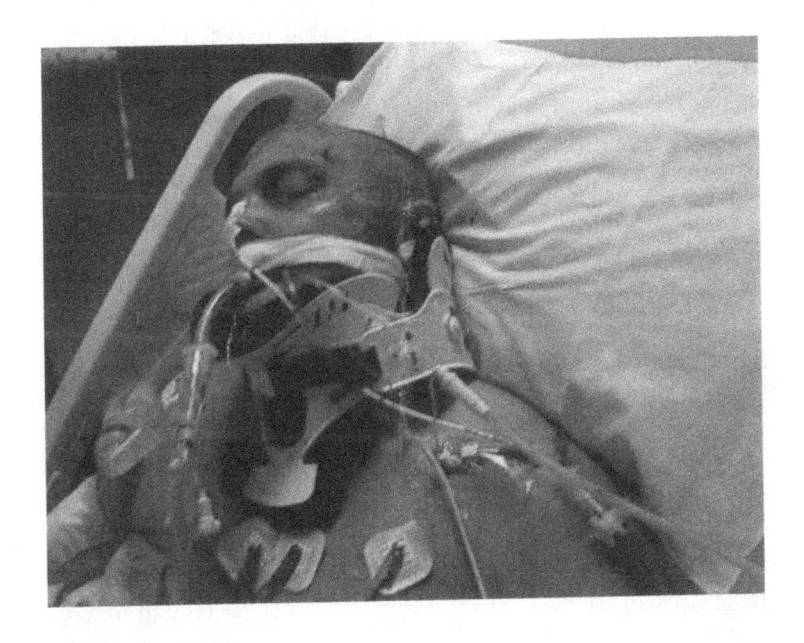

I WILL NEVER forget the day that one of the nurses in the rehabilitation hospital brought me a card that was sent to me in the mail. It was from my Grandmother Ruth, and I had no idea how much impact this card would have on my life going forward until I began reading it. My grandma was the sweetest, most caring woman that always included verses from the Bible to encourage me and point me to Jesus. I still have her card to this day because it gave me so much hope and inspiration when I was at my lowest of lows. Her inspirational message and Bible verse—"For with God, nothing will be impossible"—lit up my eyes with excitement, and the words resonated with me from that day forth (Luke 1:37, KJV). The feeling I experienced of an insurmountable hope, peace, and joy that no person or thing in this world could have given me at that instant except God will remain with me forever! To this very day, I still tell others about my breakthrough and God's mercy and grace that is available to whoever will believe and receive it through faith.

Day by day, I meditated on the promise of God that nothing would be impossible, and that things were going to continue getting better day by day. My mentality and thought process also shifted from being one of wanting to give up to one that was going to overcome through the resurrection healing power of Jesus that was inherent in all believers. The dedication to putting Jesus first place in my life, giving it my best effort in all therapies, and challenging myself to keep improving were qualities that enabled me to eventually get discharged from Brooks Rehabilitation Hospital and start readjusting to life at home. There were many disappointing and frustrating days where I felt worthless to an extent, but every time I wanted to throw in the towel, Jesus picked me back up and let me soar on wings like an eagle (Isaiah 40:31, KJV).

The final day at Brooks Rehabilitation Hospital had come, and I was looking forward to going back home and seeing what great plans God had in store for me next! After everything was cleared, along with saying our goodbyes to a lot of the staff, we were on our way to the next phase of the journey. I was happy to be home and to start the process of outpatient therapy along with getting back to some normalcy. My parents made it a point to walk with me around the neighborhood to build back endurance after being bedridden for so long. I could feel small amounts of improvement being made, but one thing that really bothered me was the left side of my body being extremely weak and not being able to fully extend my left arm above my head. During every therapy session, the physical therapist would stretch my arm and tell me things to work on, and I felt like things were going nowhere because he had no clue how I was feeling or what I had experienced with my TBI. Both he and the occupational therapist meant well in their efforts to help me recover, but they were just reading statistics from charts and using their book smarts rather than truly being able to empathize with me to see where I was coming from. This devastated me, and I quickly thought it was useless going to my therapy appointments.

After completing so many sessions and receiving clearance, I was now on my own to make any further physical and cognitive improvements. This was going to be a challenge, but I knew that "with God all things are made possible," which gave me confidence during the new storm I was about to face (Matthew 19:26, KJV). Growing up as an athlete who likes all sports with basketball being my favorite, I never felt so discouraged as I did each time I tried to shoot a basketball or catch a football. I was pathetically weak on my left side, and it was so embarrassing every time I attempted a shot or tried to make a catch and had zero strength to lift my left arm. This continued for quite a while, and I remember attempting every strength developing exercise possible for my left side. From using dumbbells to bodyweight movements and even resistance bands, I maximized every outlet with the goal in mind of regaining strength and mobility on my left side as well as total body strengthening along with conditioning.

Being a patient of Brooks Rehabilitation Hospital was a blessing because not too long after being discharged and living at home, I learned of a day program offered to TBI survivors located in Jacksonville, Florida called the Brooks Clubhouse. This environment was a good setup for me to be socially engaged with other survivors that I could relate to and to work with the staff there to help me continue making forward progress. When I started there, the manager Kathy introduced me to everyone. Not long thereafter, I became settled in and found my niche in the setting they had placed me. Completing various tasks in the morning such as maintenance activities, business related duties, or prepping the food in the kitchen were the three options members had to choose from. I chose maintenance because it involved being physically active, and the back of the house art and ceramic section really drew my interest the more I attended. Pretty ceramics, paintings, jewelry, crafts, and candles made from soy wax were just a few of the items members of the maintenance team could experiment with after the morning work duties had been completed.

Breaking midday for lunch and then resuming with cognitive games and other group activities was the normal routine at the Clubhouse. The afternoon activities that incorporated group discussions really helped me improve my communication skills along with other basic life skills needed to progress where God has brought me today. With the help of the staff asking me what I was passionate about and wanting to set goals for the future, they were able to network with some of their contacts and get me a volunteer position at the Brooks YMCA in Jacksonville, Florida. Having a passionate attitude about health, fitness, and sports, as well as wanting to go back to school to finish my degree, was part of God's plan for me. God used the people in my path to pave the way for my future courses of action.

The first time I began volunteering with the Brooks Wellness program at the YMCA gave me a sense of accomplishment and gratification like never before! Being on the giving end helping stroke survivors exercise was so rewarding, as well as seeing their appreciation and being able to empathize with them and their caregiver(s). This was the start of the more than 1600 volunteer hours that I put in with both Brooks Rehabilitation and the YMCA over several years. God truly humbled me over this time by showing me how much it meant to serve others just as Jesus did when He was living on the earth before being crucified on the cross. After working with others much less fortunate than myself, I realized how blessed I was. As time progressed, I then reached out to the Wellness Director at the Brooks YMCA to see if I could do some additional volunteering on the first level fitness floor. He agreed and was on board to have me shadow some of the personal trainers and himself at times when conducting training sessions and other assignments around the facility. This was a huge success for me and gave me lots of confidence in my abilities and skill sets, so that one day I would be able to thrive on my own in the professional setting.

I will never forget some of the connections I made through my volunteer experiences. Developing those relationships and being able to use them as contacts and references has contributed to where I am at today. For the first few years after my accident, I would reach points of extreme fatigue that caused me to want to sleep all the time. Looking back in retrospect, I praise and thank the Lord for sustaining the energy in me that was needed to successfully complete every assignment He had called me for! Even today, I still get tired occasionally and need to go to bed early every night; however, it is nothing compared to how it used to be in the beginning. Learning the necessary practical skills and being able to have a lot of social interaction while on the job was critical to my development and to where God has miraculously brought me today!

Being a volunteer as well as a member still at the Brooks Clubhouse was exciting! Things were slowly improving, and I could start to see light at the end of the tunnel. After a few more months passed, staff members at the Clubhouse thought I was ready to transition back to school with a light course load so I could eventually earn my college degree, since I never completed college during my pre-accident days. After meetings with the school, my parents and I were in the initial steps to getting me enrolled at University of North Florida to taking one non-degree related course. This was a tedious process that was frustrating, but I was able to enroll in one Health Science course for the fall semester the year of 2010. With much preparation and support from my parents, I began class with an optimistic mindset that I would learn a lot and do well. The first few classes were tough psychologically for me because I was overly concerned about what other students would think of me. This thought process continued for a while, especially when I registered with the Disability Resource Center on campus, which enabled me to have classroom accommodations for the semester.

Some of these accommodations included extra time to complete tests, quizzes, assignments, projects, and papers along with an optional notetaker. I could also take my quizzes and tests in an isolated and quiet environment to prevent disruptions and not ruin my thought process. The ticking of the clock on the wall or any slight noise in the classroom would bother me due to the brain injury, so it was necessary to receive the help from the school's Disability Resource Center. A part of me always felt guilty by using these accommodations due to the fact of another student finding out and me being embarrassed for having extra help. It took a while to put this behind me. Preparation and study time for class were difficult because I always told people that for every hour the average student spent studying or completing an assignment, it would take me two to three times as long with lots of repetition being the key to comprehending the subject material. This was very taxing on me, as I was used to being a very quick learner with a great memory. However, after suffering the TBI, it was like starting all over again. With a lot of confidence, determination, and perseverance instilled in me from God, I completed the semester with a low B for my grade and was relieved that the hard work paid off!

CHAPTER SIX

Getting Back in School Mode

NOW THAT I had completed a successful first semester in college, I felt that the possibility of me earning a degree had now become a reality. My confidence level was back up, but to be enrolled in the Health Science degree program, I had to first pass all the necessary prerequisites. Once again, I found myself back at St. Johns River Community College in St. Augustine, Florida—close to my home to start the process of completing the prerequisite courses. The spring semester began, and I was looking forward to the challenge of putting my brain to the test of passing Psychology, Microbiology, Anatomy and Physiology 1 and 2, and Chemistry. I did not take all the courses together but rather took them one semester at a time, which was more manageable due to my TBI ultimately affecting my executive functioning, caused from my frontal lobe injury.

God was on the move in my life because, shortly before I began the new semester that spring, a staff member at the Brooks Clubhouse referred me to the Department of Vocational Rehabilitation, which helped me out tremendously from that point forward with school tuition and job placement! After meeting with and being assigned a counselor, the DVR made a personalized plan to help me reach the goal of being a health science graduate and an exercise specialist. School was going well, and I developed good rapports with my professors. This helped me because I felt connected to the learning process, and it helped me to persevere by giving my best effort. Not only was I making As in all of my courses, but the practicality of the subject matter was being applied in the real-world scenarios I was faced with. I was seeing the principles being read in my studies and taught in classroom lectures occurring which helped me to retain the information better.

Every few months, I was required to check in with my DVR counselor to report my grades and discuss how things were going. Each time I would visit, my counselor could see the excitement and passion in my voice about my progress! Along with funding my school tuition, DVR also agreed to pay for all my strength and conditioning courses, which included many credentials and specializations that I have earned along the way. In the last semester of my final course to complete before returning to UNF for the Health Science degree program, I had a determination to finish strongly to be on track for the next phase of the journey. When the prerequisites were finally finished, I had a celebration with my parents before reapplying to UNF for the undergraduate health science program. This was another monumental accomplishment for me. I gave Jesus all the credit, glory, honor, and praise for getting me to where I was!

When my application to UNF was approved and I was admitted to the program, I was thrilled about the news and ready to begin! I registered for two courses at UNF at this time—two per semester after much counseling from therapists as well as those closest to me. It was an added challenge that made me manage my time better by allowing more days in between to complete assignments and study. I still had my accommodations through the Disability Resource Center, which always benefited me by taking quizzes and tests in an isolated, quiet environment in their facility. My grades were maintained at a high level, and I was able to apply the subject matter learned to real life scenarios, which was very meaningful to forward my development. Having various group related discussions and assignments throughout my time also enabled me to work on my public speaking ability, which over the long haul had improved dramatically.

Semester by semester, I kept the two-course schedule, and even though it seemed like I would never finish, God kept lighting the fire inside of me to not give up or quit. There were many ups and downs along the way of my journey to this point, but God always remained faithful. God will perfect the good work in which He started in me and each of us believers until its completion to the day of Jesus Christ (Philippians 1:6, KJV)! Getting used to a lot of the familiar faces in all my classes was a common theme since the school typically admits one cohort of students at a time that remain together throughout the program. Becoming accustomed to seeing the regulars gave me the continuity I needed to keep pushing through to the finish line. As I approached the final two semesters before graduation and having completed all the major coursework, the attention was now beginning to be shifted to potential internship and job sites for me to complete my hours. A final poster board project presentation was required at the end of the internship. All things were going fine, and it looked like my internship preceptor for the last semester would be Brooks Rehabilitation, which was a blessing from the Lord since that was where I recovered from my accident!

Upon mentioning the news regarding my internship to the manager at the Brooks Clubhouse, she was ecstatic to have someone with a TBI as a member of the program to come back and see things from a different perspective. When the forms were completed, it was set in stone that I would be returning for my final semester to be an intern for the Brooks Clubhouse. This was reassuring for me knowing that I would have this opportunity to let God's glory shine through me! Before I started the internship, the pre-internship course had to be taken to get everything organized and pass some assignments along with tests providing insight as what to expect in the last semester. At the same time, I was taking my college courses, I was enrolled with my strength and conditioning credentials. When I finished each course and earned the certification credential, I had to send a copy over to my DVR counselor as proof of completion. The second to last academic school semester was a success, and I earned an A in the pre-internship class, paving the way for my much-anticipated last semester!

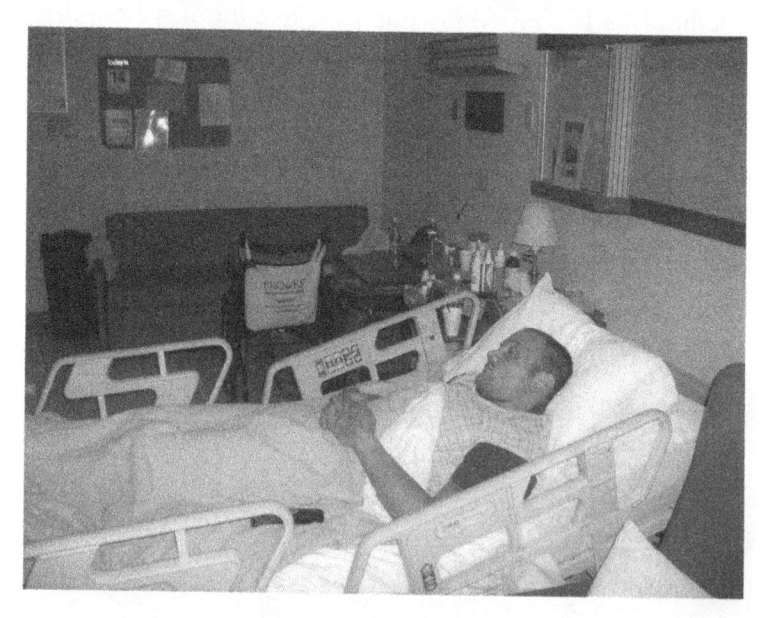

By this time in my recovery, I had been driving for a little while and was now confident in my abilities to navigate myself to the job site. My internship was split between traveling to the Brooks Clubhouse in Jacksonville, Florida twice per week and going to the St. Augustine YMCA twice per week to assist with the Brooks Wellness Program offered there. A total of 300 hours between both sites needed to be completed to graduate in December. The first day was exciting getting to see all the members at the Brooks Clubhouse, and they were proud to see me on the other side of things working as an intern. This was a special time for me considering I would now be assisting my former peers with their daily work unit assignments and helping with other various tasks during the day. My job duties at the YMCA were to help members with their workouts, chart their progress, and record blood pressure readings before and after they finished. Between the two sites, I really enjoyed what I was doing and made significant impacts on those that I worked closely with.

When I neared the end of my 300 hours, I was eager to get started on my final poster board project presentation. Gathering photos and writing the different sections to be placed on the poster board was now my focus. Reading and rereading the directions to the project was top priority as I wanted to make sure that I did the best job I could possibly do. I had finally come to the end of completing all the instructions, and it was time to go to the site on campus that would print my finished poster board so that I could have it for display. As soon as I saw the finished product, I knew that it was my time to shine at the poster board presentation ceremony! The ceremony was in the next few days, and I needed to dress business professional and answer all questions relating to my project and experience at the internship site.

CHAPTER SEVEN

Graduation and Volunteering

THE POSTER PRESENTATION ceremony was a success. I finished my undergraduate years making an A in the final internship semester. It was now time to order my cap and gown and prepare to walk on the stage and receive my diploma! The day was finally there—December 11th, 2015—and I had my parents and some relatives in the stands to support me. When I was awarded my diploma, I thanked the Lord in my heart and was incredibly grateful to be in the situation that I was! After sitting down with my graduating class in the aisles, I patiently waited until the conclusion of the ceremony when my parents summoned me to take pictures with various people to keep as memories of the special occasion. The pictures taken included some serious ones along with quite a few funny ones. My family and I gathered and then drove to a restaurant to celebrate the big day!

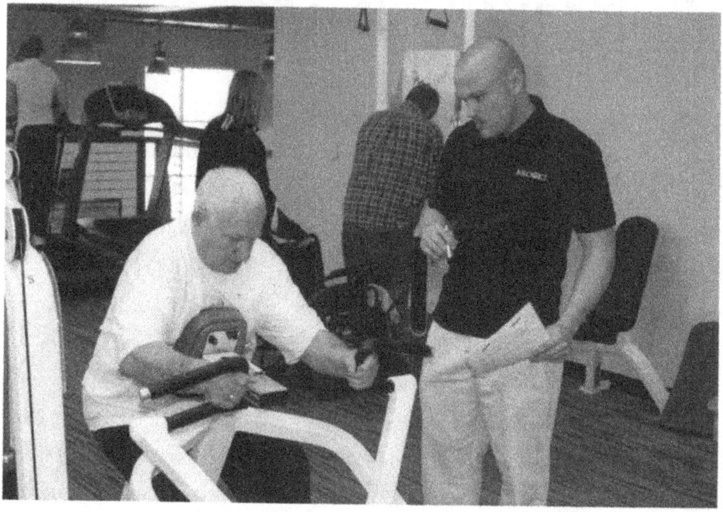

Once the reality had set in that I was a college graduate, I was looking forward to the next chapter of life that God had in store for me. My parents and I considered me continuing to volunteer with the Brooks Wellness program at the YMCA to gain more work experience. This was the best plan at the time because it gave me more confidence in my abilities to apply the knowledge I had in an environment that suited all my skills. Each time I volunteered, it was a cherished opportunity to positively encourage and inspire the people in the program. Several months had passed, and the Lord put it on my heart to pursue a Master of Health Science, as well as to keep volunteering. This thought was presented to my parents, and after much consideration, I was enrolled in the online master's in health education and promotion at Walden University. Being fresh off graduation and still currently in the "school mode," I began the first semester in February of 2016.

It was not long into the program when I realized it was going to be much more challenging and require a lot better time management skills than my undergraduate studies did. I was ready for the challenge and the dedication it would take to complete the degree successfully! Several months went by, and I felt confident in my abilities to manage all the coursework in each course I took. The program required fifty credit hours to be earned to receive the degree. My schedule was set, having me take one five credit hour course each term, and the entire program would take me around two and a half years to finish. Things were off to a great start, and I was still able to manage volunteering three days per week with the Brooks Wellness program at the YMCA for a total of twelve hours per week.

My grades were kept up, and I was retaining the information in ways that were beneficial to my continued success in the health field. Being able to recognize and apply principles from my studies to my volunteer experience along with everyday life was a psychological boost for me at the time. Overall, I could feel the work in my spirit that only God could do in me! Setting aside enough time to complete all assignments, papers, group work, projects, quizzes, and tests I had was difficult, but it taught me the importance of time management and being able to prioritize certain things over others. There were weekly modules to complete with a list of the work to submit by the deadline, and if there was a project or paper due in the future, the student had the opportunity to get a head start on it. Many times, I took advantage of this so that I would not need to cram it in or rush to finish it at the last minute. Pacing myself throughout the terms was vital to my forward progress and success in the program.

When I was halfway through with the program, my parents, DVR counselor, and I thought it would be worthwhile for me to look for employment while going to school to see if it would work. I was excited because this would be my chance to shine in an environment that I am highly passionate about! It would give me more responsibility and a sense of accomplishment by being able to balance both during the same time. I began putting out applications to numerous gyms and health clubs, and for the longest time things remained silent without hearing back from any of the organizations. This was a tough time for me, as it was hard on my emotions and my sense of self-worth. I was professionally qualified, had put in the time with lots of experience, and was ready to make a positive impact with whomever selected me. As more time went by without hearing from anyone, my DVR counselor made a good decision in giving me a job coach to help me find and retain employment.

Not long after being supported by the job coach, my first response came in from LA Fitness. The personal training director called me for a phone interview and our conversation lasted for quite a while with it all going well! He finished our talk by asking me to come to the gym for an in-person interview with him. Things were the same with my school and volunteering, but if I were hired at LA Fitness, I would have to give notice to my supervisor at the YMCA to tell them my volunteer duties would be coming to an end. The day had arrived for my in-person interview, and I was prepared to make a good first impression to be hired. We talked at his desk for a for a little while, and after a relatively short interview compared to our phone conversation, I was hired! He then gave me a tour around the facility introducing me to the other personal trainers and staff. I was now officially hired on as a master trainer because of all my certifications, specializations, and work experience! Before exiting, the personal training director told me he would contact me when they had received my background check paperwork for clearance.

Knowing that I was hired as a master personal trainer was fantastic news, and I praised and thanked God for opening the door for employment! During this time, I still had about three or four courses left to complete before earning my master's degree. Not many days after the interview process, I was contacted by the personal training director and told to start now because the paperwork had been cleared. I made it known to my volunteer supervisor that I was hired elsewhere and would no longer be coming. She was happy for me and wished me well!

I will never forget the day I started the job—November 29th, 2017—because it was my dad's birthday!

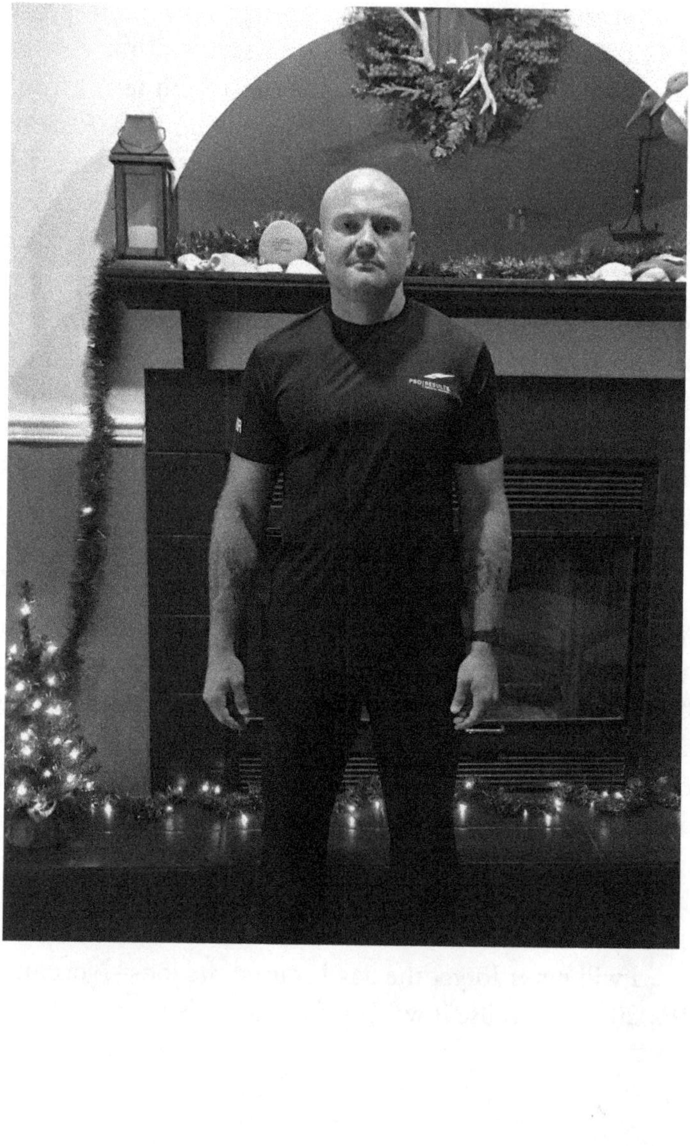

CHAPTER EIGHT

Master's Degree and Work

THE FIRST SEVERAL weeks of my new job were tough because I had not yet built up a client list and was just beginning to learn the process. I had an important paper due in school, a few other assignments, and the responsibility of learning the names of my coworkers as well as the regular members I got used to seeing at the gym. Even though things were slow for me at work in the early stages, my mind was determined to do a great job between balancing work and school. The nice part about being a master personal trainer at LA Fitness is that my director did all the marketing and sold personal training packages to numerous people so that the trainers could focus strictly on working with their clients. As I became more comfortable over time, my client list included my first two people I would begin giving training sessions to.

My professor returned our graded papers with comments, and I was elated over my grade along with the encouraging words written regarding the content of my work! At that very second, I praised Jesus in my heart, thanking Him for giving me the ability to perform at a high level on a difficult paper! The first two clients of mine at work were a blessing to train because they both had some limitations that I needed to be aware of when designing their exercise programs. They were happy to work with me, and over time, they were making significant progress working towards attaining their specific goals. Things were moving in the right direction, and I was incredibly joyful to have been where God had brought me!

With only two courses remaining before earning my master's degree, business was starting to gradually pick up for me at work. I needed to maintain focus at strongly finishing my graduate degree. Preparation ahead of training sessions with my clients was always done to give me an exact blueprint of how I would go about their individual workouts. I would get teased a lot by the other trainers when they saw me take client books home, as they would laugh thinking that I was always doing my "homework assignments." This may have been the case, but with a TBI, it was the only way I knew that would prepare me and help retain the information needed to give quality training sessions to my clients. Juggling the information from school and then putting into practice at work became the best of both worlds for me, as I saw the principles being taught applied in real life scenarios. At this point in time, I was confident in my ability to do well in school and at work!

Slowly more clients kept filling up my schedule, and I was enthusiastic to meet them and design a program that would customize their needs along with future goals. My personality was one which gets along fine with anyone of all ages, ability levels, and backgrounds. Most of my clients were middle aged men and women, along with a lot of senior citizens. I tended to gravitate towards this group because of my caring, empathetic attitude, which was strongly correlated with my accident and the tough times I faced in recovery.

It was a strange situation because, prior to my accident, I wanted nothing to do with the elderly or people outside of my own age bracket. God had done a miraculous work in my life of humbling me to a point where I could recognize the hurt and pain someone might have been going through—a lot more today than I could before.

The second to last course was now completed with me earning another A, and I had a cumulative GPA of close to 3.5! I had one course left to pass before earning my master's degree in the fall of 2018, and now that business at work had picked up for me, it was time to really focus on reaching the end goal of graduation. After checking the online syllabus for the next term and preparing for some upcoming major projects, I then set aside time to organize exercise plans for my clients, which involved a lot of dedication to devote quality time to each category. There was no doubt that the next few months were going to be an uphill battle for me, but I knew in my heart that God had given me the strength to endure it and come out successful!

Having worked with athletes, people with disabilities, seniors, youth, and pretty much every possibility you can think of, I was now in my element at work due to my previous experiences and knowledge in the profession. I was more comfortable giving my clients great workouts and was receiving phenomenal feedback from them! Having to complete a fifteen-page paper and a major project putting together all the information I had learned in the program were the last two big grades of the course to go, along with less weighted assignments, quizzes, and tests. My clients were all nice people who really appreciated the quality help and time I gave them. Knowing that my services were valued and effectively working among my clientele, I was inspired and motivated to excel in the last academic term before graduation, which was only several weeks away!

My own physical health and wellness had come a long way from the very beginning stages after my accident. The Lord restored me to peak physical condition, which I was so blessed and grateful for! This progression contributed to the academic success as well as with the positive social interactions at work with clients, co-workers, and my director. My self-esteem level was high, and this was an important factor that helped me feel confident when preparing my papers, projects, and assignments for school. Having my job at the same time as being a student was a humbling experience because it gave me a real sense of accomplishment. Dedicating time to organize the framework of both my paper and project was something that I got a head start on because they were both going to be challenging to compose. Reading the instructions many times before starting was needed so that I would clearly comprehend the exact specifications the professor was looking for. Initially when I first started back to school after my accident, it was very frustrating having to repeat things over and over for memory retention, but over time I greatly improved!

My rough draft outlines for the paper and project were now ready, and this was crucial as my clientele list was gradually increasing. I really enjoyed the work I did helping clients work harder and smarter to see better versions of themselves! Many of my clients knew that I was completing my master's degree while working, and they were all proud of me! Doing the research for the work was tedious, but it was all rewarding for me in the long run as it taught me how to better use search mechanisms to navigate through the information when not sure where to start. All the hard work up until now was not going to go to waste because I was set on finishing strong with my diploma as the reward to look forward to! Successful client experiences and maintaining the retention of all clients from day one was a blessing from God to go along with excelling in school! The time had come when I submitted my final drafts to the professor and now only had a few minor assignments left in the next two weeks to finish before waiting on my final grade and graduation announcements.

It was the end of summer in late August 2018, and it was any day now which my grades would be revealed for the major assignments I completed, as well as the final grade for the semester. I was eager to see the results because I knew that the effort and time spent on my part was going to produce a great finish! Every week in my school account email inbox I would receive emails regarding checking in with your academic counselor to determine if you were eligible for graduation. For me, it all depended on earning a passing grade in the last class, as I already knew from prior communication that my eligibility for graduation was on track assuming successful completion of the final course. After earning a B in the class, I was jumping with joy praising Jesus! I finished with a 3.4 GPA, along with a Master of Science in Health Education and Promotion degree!

Walden University
Having completed the studies and satisfied the requirements prescribed by the Board of Directors of Walden University
Beau Baker
is conferred the degree of
Master of Science
in
Health Education and Promotion
WALDEN UNIVERSITY
University of North Florida
Beau James Baker
Bachelor of Science in Health

Graduating with my master's degree was a huge accomplishment that I give all the credit, glory, honor, and praise to God because He gave me the ability and mental focus to be able to finish strongly! Looking back on my progress over the years since my accident, this was a major milestone with the Lord receiving all the accolades, and I was the blessed recipient of a wonderful season of two and a half years in my life, earning a master's degree while working! This was all valuable experience, as it had given me a better perspective on life and the things that many of us overlook and take for granted. From the achievements with school and work giving me more self-confidence, the real transformation came from within my heart. Jesus took a hold of me and was first place in every area, and I began to see everything else transcend to a higher level!

CHAPTER NINE

Success at Work and Personal Life

THE CLIENT LIST was continuing to expand, and I had now accumulated more than thirty clients since the start of my employment. It was a pleasure going to work and having a variety of conditions to oversee, as well as helping everyone get a better grip on their health and wellness by coaching them the best ways I possibly could! The biggest reward taken away from my experience as a master personal trainer was the appreciation seen in the faces of my clients as well as knowing they were working hard to make positive changes. As in anything, some people worked harder than others, but at the end of the day, the perseverance and desire to never give up even when life got tough was the attitude I tried to instill in all my clients. This happened regardless of their exercise history or disability handicaps they may have had.

> For with God **nothing** shall be impossible.
>
> –Luke 1:37

GOD WILL MAKE A WAY WHERE THERE SEEMS TO BE NO WAY.

Personally, I was seeing God's hand move in my life, which sometimes did not seem comprehensible. However, knowing that with God all things are possible as well as with God, nothing will be impossible gave me the continued hope I needed to keep pressing forward (Matthew 19:26, KJV; Luke 1:37, KJV). Not a single day goes by that I am reluctant to give Jesus honor and praise because of His ultimate sacrifice on the cross for us, as well as His goodness and mercy that keeps chasing after me regardless of all my faults! At the onset of my recovery, when it seemed like all hope was lost, God stepped in on the scene to give me His breath of abundant life, which has never dissipated and only continues to expand more and more with each passing day! My physical strength levels which were nonexistent in Brooks Hospital have now come back, with me having full range of motion in both sides of my body as well as my cognitive perception returning. Things that require a lot of physical exertion I thought would not happen anymore after my accident were now beginning to take place again, which put a smile on my face and in my heart! My favorite sport of basketball was now able to resume without any limitations and having the strength to get the ball to the rim was no longer a struggle!

Every two years, I am required to update my personal training and CPR/AED certification by taking continuing education courses to renew them. My director at work made this known to me as well as an email notification from the National Academy of Sports Medicine, with who I am accredited with. Being an organized person, my mind was set on taking a continuing education course and signing up for a CPR/AED course at the local hospital with the American Heart Association to become updated in the system. Within a few weeks, I had finished my task of renewal within the organization and was cleared by my director at work. I found that the knowledge I had attained from my master's degree program was paying off dividends to the practical applications being witnessed at work. Even in my own personal life, I was able to relate terminology learned from studying to everyday examples seen on a regular basis. This was valuable, as it certainly gave me a well-rounded, kinesthetic approach that best suited my style of learning. Being able to correlate information processed from one setting to another is an awesome quality that God has blessed me with!

Now that I was recertified with my personal training credential and had completed my master's degree, there was a small sigh of relief as the bulk of the work was now finished. However, continuing education has always been important to me because having updated facts pertaining to the field you are working in is imperative. Going to work doing something you love and have a passion for is extremely rewarding, and most people are not able to say they are excited to go to their job every day. A pattern of gradual increase in clientele began late 2018, and I was eager to meet the new clients to get them on track for their workout programs!

I am now living the reality of helping people in an environment that inspires me to be the best I can be by positively encouraging every client! Ever since the volunteer days with Brooks Rehabilitation and the YMCA, being an uplifting person has come naturally to me because God has given me a calling to be caring, empathetic, and have a relatable heart that is able to connect with whomever He puts in my path to help.

In between going to work and living everyday life, I was consistently getting my workouts in to stay strong and keep improving. Going to the gym three times a week to lift weights with the other four days devoted to cardio/conditioning and abdominal/core work was the typical routine

I followed unless something came up. Having come a long way from the initial recovery days following my accident, it was a complete turnaround from the beginning, and the strength that has been reinvigorated into me all comes from the glory of the Lord Jesus Christ! There were plenty of times when I got down and became frustrated with myself for not being able to do something or not being strong enough yet, but God gave me His strength day by day to keep pressing forward towards the purpose He has for my life. Some advice to share would be to never give up or quit on yourself or the dreams you may have.

As a Christian and believer, I learned God answers in three ways! He says yes and gives you what you want, He says no and gives you something better, He says wait and gives you the best! Whether or not you are a believer and follower of Jesus Christ, God loves everyone unconditionally. God has the best plan in store for your life, and if we trust Him, He will always come through!

Throughout the year 2019, work was incredible because I genuinely enjoyed every second spent helping my clients with their health and fitness/wellness status! The fact that most of my clientele were senior citizens was gratifying because many of them were coming off some type of injury or already had pre-existing conditions to be aware of. Some of the most rewarding times were days when many of my clients would come in telling me they did not feel like exercising, but after we got in the swing of things with our routines, they would leave the gym with huge smiles on their faces! When this occurred, it really touched me knowing that a little bit of exercise done the right way could brighten a person's day!

Towards the end of 2019 in December, my dad and I traveled to Miami, Florida to watch an NBA basketball game between the LA Lakers and the Miami Heat. Since basketball is my favorite sport and my favorite team would be playing, it was a special Christmas gift to have great tickets for this specific game, and I was extremely excited to attend! Upon arrival at the hotel, we put our belongings in the room, got ready, and walked over to the arena. Our seats were on the first level directly behind my favorite team's bench about twelve rows up, and it was an awesome experience. I will never forget my team winning the game! We also had family that lives in South Florida; so, we were able to stop in on the way home to see some of them, which was a good feeling having been able to coordinate everything in the one trip. I thought that was a special way to close out the year of 2019!

With the health and fitness industry typically seeing lots of new member sign ups at gyms due to New Year's resolutions, along with clients interested in personal training to start 2020, it was going to be a great start to the New Year as most people predicted. Yet not long into the new decade was a global pandemic that has since taken over the world. The pandemonium over a virus has frantically swept over the entire nation, leaving many hesitant to put themselves out in public places because of the spread. Labeled as the coronavirus or COVID-19, its effects forced a national shutdown for quite some time.

On March 16th, 2020, I was at work when suddenly, the news was spread throughout that the facility would be closing until further notice. I still had several clients left to train on my schedule for the day, and this was shocking news to hear of. As soon as members were notified and signs were posted, I walked to my car and drove home for the last time. Being out of work and forced to go on furlough was the only option, and I patiently waited for the government to announce lockdowns ending.

With the quarantine and self-isolation protocol, it has been a struggle to adapt to the "new normal" that has been implemented by the CDC. However, I have found this period to be a blessing in disguise, giving me more time to focus on God and fine tune the areas of my life that need improvement. Having many months to brainstorm new exercise programs for both myself and my clients, as well as spending quality time in the Bible and prayer with the Lord, have been areas that I am grateful for! Although many people would classify 2020 as a year to forget, I would disagree, saying it has been a year to reflect upon all the amazing things God has done in my life and yours too if you are a believer!

After many months passed and COVID-19 cases were growing nationwide, I decided to take an indefinite leave of absence from work even though they reopened with strict guidelines to follow. The reason for this decision is because I live with my elderly parents; my mother has lupus, so this was done out of respect for them. Business was terribly slow, and I heard people were extremely cautious about going to public environments, especially gym settings where everyone touched the equipment, spread germs if they were asymptomatic, or neglected to wear face masks properly by not covering their noses—and in some cases pulling them down all the way to breathe. Most of my elderly clients contacted me and said they were not going to return to the gym, and therefore, I would lose them as clients at LA Fitness. For these reasons and the fact that my director contracted the virus himself, I felt like these were all valid points for me to stay home until further notice. It all worked out nicely because most of my clients, no matter their age, stated they would not consider returning to the gym until 2021 or when a vaccine for the virus was developed. This gave me reassurance knowing that I would not be missing much, and the time spent at home would be quality based as I was determined to make the best of it!

CHAPTER TEN

COVID-19 and a New Venture

MY DECISION TO remain at home ended up being a good choice because, during the months of quarantine from COVID-19, I have had the opportunity to think about many things. One thing that my parents and I thought of was for me to start my own mobile personal training business to meet the needs of those who are hesitant of going back to the gym setting. Having enough time to brainstorm a lot of functional exercises, along with the knowledge base and practical experience I have, made this a real possibility. Another excellent idea my dad came up with was me being a motivational speaker, talking about my accident, and giving hope as well as inspiration to others! This could include speaking to teenagers, church members, as well as anyone with an addiction who did not believe there was hope for recovery from an addiction. My new testimony may help stop teens from drinking alcohol, stop anyone from drinking and driving, help someone facing an addiction, whether a believer or an unbeliever, or simply share with other Christians my miraculous new beginning in life.

Once the ideas were finalized, we took the next steps by ordering business cards, obtaining a business license, and setting up some sites on the internet for marketing. As with any new business venture, it usually takes time to get things moving in the right direction, and my case fell into that category. I was blessed by God in the beginning as my first client turned out to be someone who I had previously had as a client at LA Fitness before the lockdown! He was a great person and someone who I really connected with and saw lots of progress, as well as potential, in my time working with him. Getting started with a familiar face was encouraging for me, and it made the first session of my mobile personal training career a success!

Getting clients has been a struggle so far, but I am confident that in God's perfect timing they will start coming one by one. Having patience in the Lord and taking baby steps forward, my mobile training business will grow. My current client has been training with me for a few months now and has really liked the new style of in-home workouts! He has spread the word about me to several of his neighbors and passed some of my business cards out. In the meantime, to stay active and keep my mind busy, I have been group training my mom and dad at home. Just like any other client(s), I had them tell me their goals as well as any conditions or limitations to be aware of when designing specific exercise programs for them. They have worked well together, and I am proud of the improvements they have made so far!

I have continued with my workout regimen, writing this book, and studying for another major credential I am hoping to earn soon, which is the Certified Strength and Conditioning Specialist (CSCS) through the National Strength and Conditioning Association (NSCA). Composing this book has been somewhat therapeutic for me because it has given me the chance to reflect on all the amazing and miraculous things the Lord has done for me! Working out at home has helped me become more creative with exercise design, which has bettered my own routine along with giving me countless ideas of ways to implement new things for my clients. I am believing God in the matchless, mighty name of Jesus that the rest of 2021 and going forward is going to be spectacular!

While many people feel they may have lost over this year due to the pandemic, I feel that I have gained a tremendous amount of insight and revelational wisdom from God leading me on His perfect path of righteousness and success for my life. Taking a little detour by being innovative has been the spark I needed to keep pressing forward! I know that my time will come to shine as far as motivational speaking goes, and it will be done all for the glory and honor of God, not myself. While most of the world is living in fear and panic, I am choosing to praise God and believe that breakthrough will be coming soon in my life for the things I have been hoping for!

As new vaccines for the virus are being developed, there is still doubt and uncertainty for many people worldwide as to what the efficacy rate will be. Every day that I can remember back from my initial recovery period has been a slow process to get to where God has delivered me currently. The correlation between the slow process that the Lord has delivered me through and the doubt and uncertainty as to what the efficacy rate for COVID-19 will be is based on faith. Just as people can believe for positive results from the vaccine, I too have believed for greater things from God such as my healing, strength for every day, and hope for the future. Over the slow process of delivery, God has never failed me yet! The only option of dwelling on negativity and skepticism is a positional stance that will ultimately lead to disappointment and frustration, and I do not want any more of those feelings in my life!

Preparing for the upcoming seasonal harvest of an increase in new clientele for my business is the direction I have been anticipating. Once things are up and running, it will be a joy to use all the gifts the Lord has blessed me with to help as many clients as possible all for His honor and glory forever!

CHAPTER ELEVEN

Hopes for the Future

AT ONE POINT after my accident occurred (9/18/09), the only hope and wish I had was to heal and make improvement after the traumatic impact on my body. When Jesus met me right where I was in Brooks Rehabilitation Hospital, I was a mess that was broken, empty, lost, and hopeless until the day I received my grandmother's card, which significantly changed the path of my recovery process. As mentioned previously, the words in the card, along with the Bible verse, made a lasting impact on my heart. Luke 1:37 (KJV) says, "For with God nothing shall be impossible"; this verse has carried me over the years to where I currently stand today!

With the Lord's goodness, kindness, mercy, and grace, I have been able to make slow progressions over the years that have been life changing. The great news is that God has a phenomenal plan for my life and every other person that puts their faith, hope, and trust in Jesus Christ! He has a good plan for each of our lives, a purpose, and a destiny that declares a future and a hope for us as believers (Jeremiah 29:11, KJV). This scripture excites me with a joy that is incomprehensible according to the world's standards! Living every day for Jesus

Christ has been rewarding, and even though I have made a ton of mistakes along the way, I am thankful that we serve a loving and forgiving God!

To go along with my academic background knowledge in public health and health education, I believe that combing the health and fitness knowledge and skills gained over the years with all my certifications and specializations will propel me into a successful career of helping people. The goal of starting my own business is now a reality. Moving forward, it will continue to expand serving clients with the overall purpose of improving the health and wellness of every individual regardless of age, ability level, disability/handicap, or any other limitations they may have that would discourage them from starting on their fitness journey. Properly advertising my services with good marketing strategies in mind is a process goal or work in progress goal along the way, which will ultimately contribute to reaching the long-term outcome goal of positively changing the lives of all my clients. Having gained the valuable experience working at a gym as big as LA Fitness has given me a confidence and determination that my new business venture along with the motivational speaking will be a success if I keep putting God first in every area of my life as well as praising and thanking Him for everything along the way!

Other goals and hopes for the future include serving God my whole life, doing whatever He assigns me, maintaining a successful career as a public health educator/health and fitness professional, getting married, and having a family. Those are the major things listed, and all the other things will come along the way. I want to encourage, motivate, and inspire people to never give up or quit on their dreams and to remain optimistic through the challenging times in life. Doing this in person by speaking to groups of people is a goal I have for myself soon that will coincide with my mobile fitness training business. Little by little, God will use me in ways that will ultimately magnify Him through the power of His Son Jesus Christ living in my heart!

Knowing that I am not of this world and made in the likeness and image of God has given me a living hope that no one can take away! My life drifted for many years far from the Lord as I chose my own detour to travel on that almost led to my death. From where I started to where I am now, my heart rejoices with thanksgiving just at the thought of my miraculous recovery, and all the credit goes to King Jesus! I know if I continue believing in the promises of God, standing firm in my faith, having unshakeable trust, not looking back, being a prisoner of hope in Jesus, and waiting patiently that the Lord will never let me down, disappoint, or fail me. I will leave you with this scripture that God commanded Moses to tell the Israelites when he led them out of Egypt.

> And Moses said to the people, "Do not be afraid. Stand still, and see the salvation of the LORD, which He will accomplish for you today. For the Egyptians whom you see today, you shall see again no more forever. The LORD will fight for you, and you shall hold your peace."
> —Exodus 14:13-14, KJV

CONCLUSION

HAVING READ THROUGH my story, you should now have a better understanding of what a TBI (traumatic brain injury) is and the significant impacts it comes with. I am very blessed and fortunate to have come out of my auto accident the way I have, because many people in similar circumstances are not able to say the same. God put all the right medical professionals in my life in His perfect timing, and I will always be forever grateful, giving my Lord and Savior Jesus Christ all the credit, praise, glory, and honor!

Being aware of people with disabilities and how to use proper etiquette when around the target population is of importance. Knowing the individual for who they are and special qualities they possess is crucial for their continued growth and progress. Anyone living with a TBI, including myself, will tell you that emotional support from care givers and loved ones makes a big difference. Instead of labeling us as mentally challenged, retarded, and slow people, we all should have more respect and understand everything about the injury before drawing conclusions.

I personally want to thank you for taking the time to read through my story! Now that you are a little more educated about TBI, the opportunities are there in case you ever cross paths with another survivor to engage in conversation with them or volunteer your time with various groups and rehabilitation facilities. As it is for me a survivor, I hope the same is true for you when it comes to the humble attitude experienced when interacting with TBI survivors. Go out into your community and make a difference in the lives of people with disabilities by giving them a smile, saying hello, or, most importantly, showing them that you genuinely care!

ABOUT THE AUTHOR

BEAU BAKER IS a survivor of a near fatal, life-changing automobile accident that left him with a TBI (traumatic brain injury). He is alive and well today, sharing the events that led up to the traumatic experience and The Only Way (Jesus Christ) he believes his life has been restored. After doctors initially gave him less than four hours to live with the best scenario, he would live in a vegetative state; he then later went on to earn both his bachelor's and master's degrees in public health/health education. Beau has accomplished much spiritually, academically, and athletically.

Being introverted due to social anxiety disorder along with obsessive compulsive disorder, which is what led Beau to start drinking alcohol. His wanting to open up and be the social butterfly amongst his peers led to the poor choices he made. He has been sober since the accident (9/18/09) and gives all the honor and glory to God!

Beau is an inspiration to others by helping them live "happier/healthier" lives through the work he does as a health and fitness coach and by his testimony. He is passionate about what he does and is excited to keep moving forward with the great plan God has for his life. Although Beau lives with a traumatic brain injury compiled with OCD, he has been abundantly blessed. The purpose of this book is to give encouragement and hope to those who may be struggling, wanting to give up, or just needing an extra boost of motivation to keep on going!

Printed in the USA
CPSIA information can be obtained
at www.ICGtesting.com
LVHW040526100424
776957LV00001B/155

9 781637 692684